WARRIOR

A portion of book sales have been donated to

The Smush Foundation.

Thank you for supporting animal welfare.

For Lindsey and Laura, who never gave up.

respect cats.

they will teach you how to live.

taking care of yourself first
is different than being selfish.
remember that.
you are no good for anyone else
if you are running on empty.

every day is a new day to begin again.
don't give up.

be original.

the world has too many copycats.

don't let anyone tell you who you are.
that is your job. be real.

life is an adventure! enjoy the little things!
gratitude lists help. they really do!

no one can be happy all the time. it's okay. embrace every part of yourself and move through the waves of emotion.

be proud of how far you've come.

pay it forward and always give back when you can.

stand up for what you believe in even if no one stands with you. your voice is important.

Life is short.
Play hard.
Be kind.
Live honestly.
Eat the bread.

never give up. life is beautiful.

CPSIA information can be obtained
at www.ICGtesting.com
Printed in the USA
BVHW021812120321
602397BV00015B/137